Amanda's Fire Drill

A Book about Fire Safety

by Kerry Dinmont

Published by The Child's World®
1980 Lookout Drive • Mankato, MN 56003-1705
800-599-READ • www.childsworld.com

ISBN 9781503820364
LCCN 2016960942

Printed in the United States of America
PA02340

Amanda and her class have a fire **drill** today.

How do they practice
fire safety?

Fire escape routes

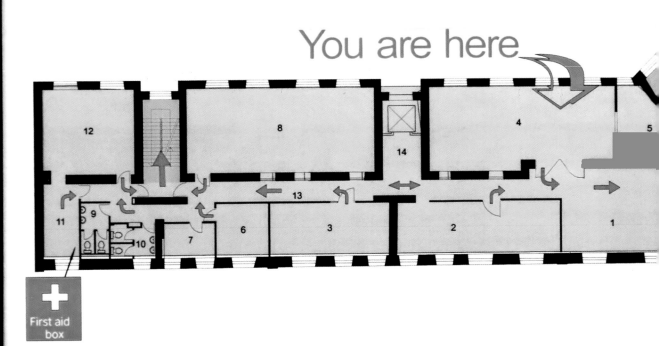

You are here

First aid box

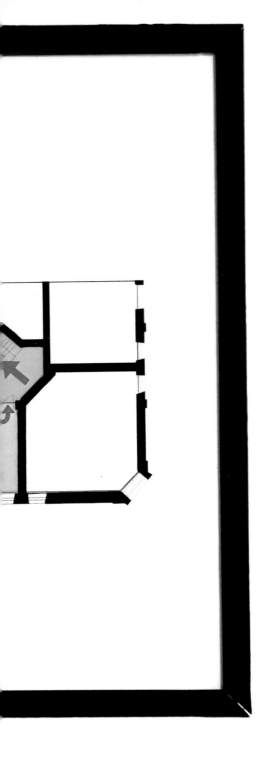

A map is in Amanda's classroom. It shows the fire escape **routes** from her classroom.

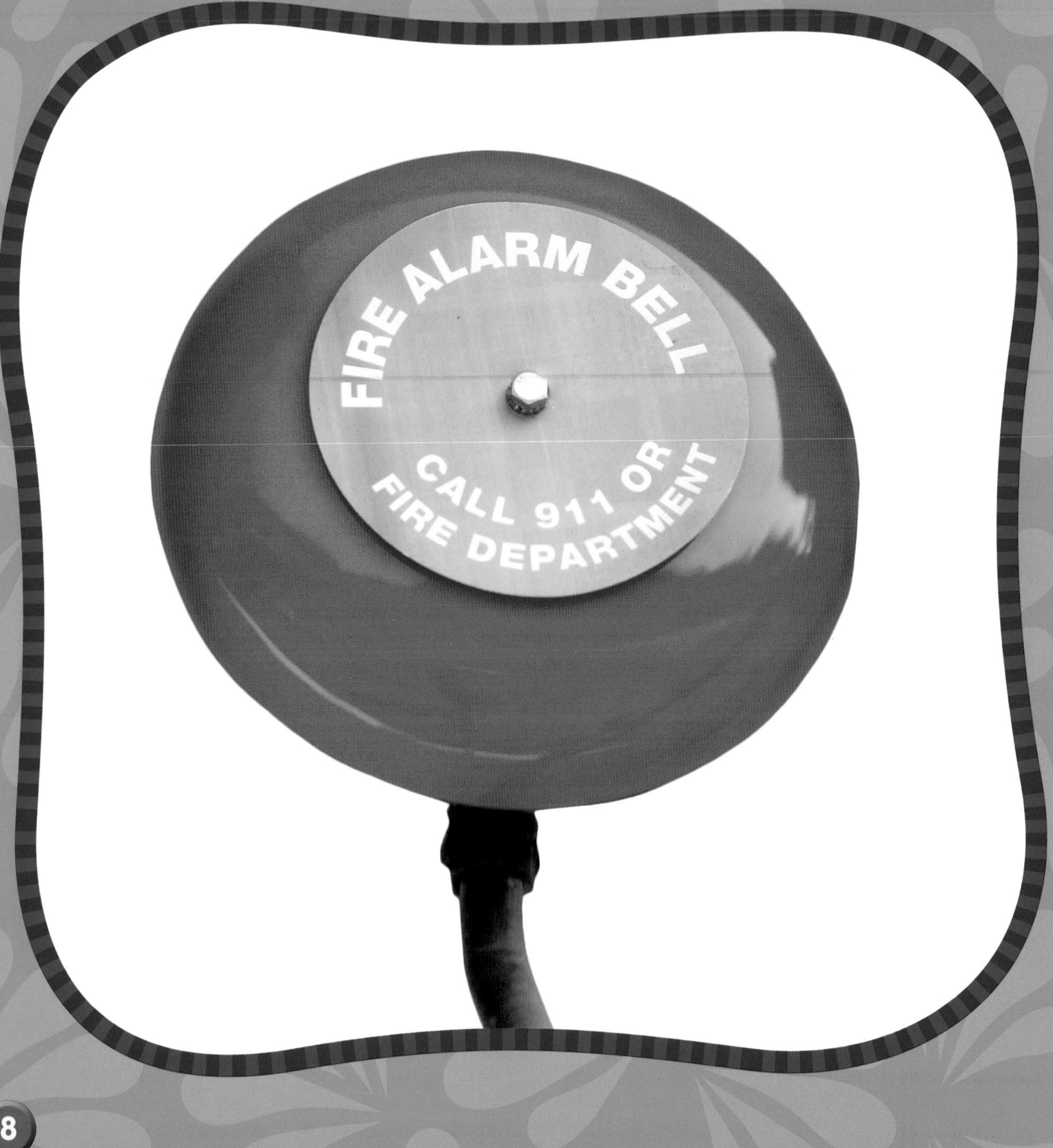
FIRE ALARM BELL
CALL 911 OR
FIRE DEPARTMENT

The fire alarm rings.
Amanda and the class
pretend it is real.

The class lines up.
The students need to
get outside quickly.

Amanda stays quiet and calm. She listens to her teacher's instructions.

The teacher checks the door handle. It is cool. She walks the class out the door.

The teacher tells them they should crawl if there is a real fire. Smoke rises. It would be higher in the air.

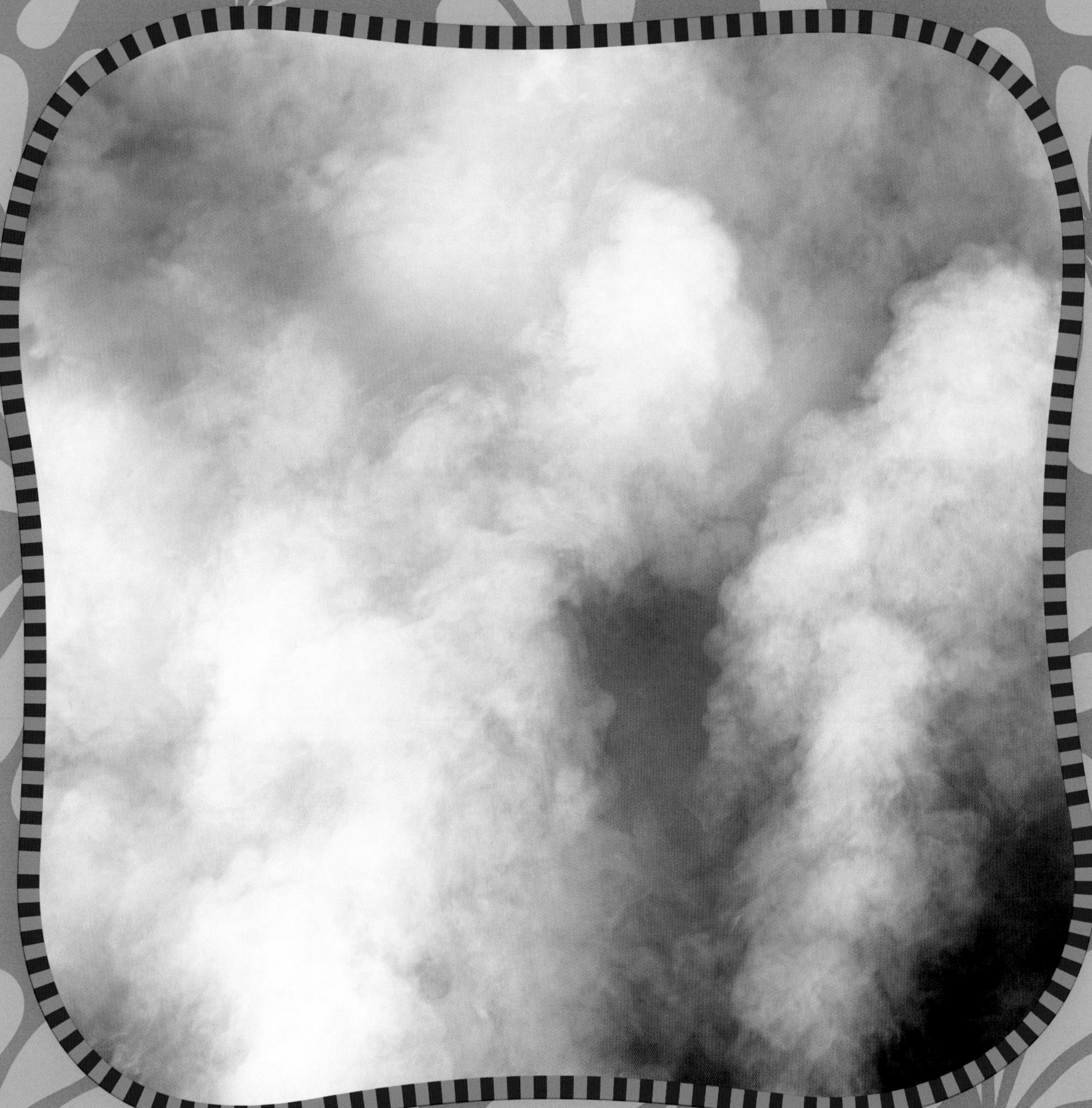

They go to a safe place outside. Amanda's class waits at the playground.

Do you know what to do if there is a fire?

Glossary

drill (DRIL) A drill is a practice of what to do in an emergency. Amanda practices a fire drill to learn what to do if there is a real fire.

routes (ROWTS) Routes are paths. Escape routes show how to get out of a building in an emergency.

Extended Learning Activities

1. Think of a time you have done a fire drill. What route did you take to get out of the building?

2. How do you practice fire safety in your home?

3. What other kinds of emergencies do you have drills for in school?

To Learn More

Books

Herrington, Lisa M. *Fire Safety*.
New York, NY: Children's Press, 2012.

Kesselring, Susan. *Being Safe with Fire*.
Mankato, MN: The Child's World, 2011.

Web Sites

Visit our Web site for links about fire safety:
childsworld.com/links

Note to Parents, Teachers, and Librarians: We routinely verify our Web links to make sure they are safe and active sites. So encourage your readers to check them out!

About the Author

Kerry Dinmont is a children's book author who enjoys art and nature. She lives in Montana with her two Norwegian elkhounds.